POCKET BABIES

By Katherine McGlade Marko

A FIRST BOOK

FRANKLIN WATTS
A Division of Grolier Publishing
New York / London / Hong Kong / Sydney
Danbury, Connecticut

Cover photographs copyright ©: Animals Animals (Jim Tuten).

Photographs copyright ©: Tom J. Ulrich: p.6; Animals Animals: pp. 8 top (Partridge Films Limited/OSF), 8 bottom, 36, 47 (all Hans & Judy Beste), 19 (Mike & Elvan Habight), 21, 22 (both R. K. LaVal), 24 (Jim Tuten), 32, 58 (both A. G. Wells/OSF), 39, 52 (both Fritz Prenzel); Visuals Unlimited: pp. 10 (Steve Maslowski), 13, 14 (John D. Cunningham), 34 (J. Alcoch), 51 (Rich Riski); Photo Researchers, Inc.: pp. 16 (Steve Maslowski), 26 (R. Van Nostrand), 29 (Peter Skinner), 35, 45 (both Tom McHugh), 37 (Kjell B. Sandved), 49 (Michael McCoy); The Wildlife Collection: p. 43 (Dean Lee); Gerry Ellis Nature Photography: pp. 54,56.

Library of Congress Cataloging-in-Publication Data

Marko, Katherine.
    Pocket babies / by Katherine McGlade Marko
       p.   cm. — (A First book)
    Includes bibliographical references and index.
    Summary: Examines marsupials, those animals that carry their babies
    in pouches, including the opossum, kangaroo, and Tasmanian devil.
    ISBN 0-531-20211-9
    1. Marsupialia — Juvenile literature. 2 Marsupialia —Infancy —Juvenile
    literature. [1. Marsupials.] I. Title. II. Series.
    QL737. M3M29 1995
    599.2—dc20   95-9542 CIP AC

Contents

A Menagerie of Pocket Babies

A mother kangaroo hops along with her baby tucked safely in her front pocket. Baby peeks out, looking around at the world. If you have ever been lucky enough to see such a sight, you may have wondered about that pocket. What a strange and wonderful thing it is, keeping mother and baby close and warm.

Many fascinating animals besides kangaroos carry their babies in pockets. They all belong to a group of animals called *marsupials,* which comes from the Latin word *marsupium,* meaning "pouch." There are more than two hundred species of mar-

A baby wallaby, a kind of kangaroo, is snuggled in its mother's pocket.

supials. Seventy of those species, almost all of them opossums, live in North, Central, and South America. All other marsupials are inhabitants of Australia and nearby islands. These exotic creatures usually have delightful names, such as wallaby, wombat, bandicoot, wallaroo, and boodie. Many of them were named by the natives of Australia, who are called *aborigines.*

Marsupials range in size from little pouched mice to the largest of all, the kangaroos. Some are like cats, some like wolves, and others like rabbits. The adorable koala is like a small bear. Most pocket babies are friendly and affectionate, but a few, such as the Tasmanian devil, can be dangerous.

Some are plant-eating, or *herbivorous,* and others are meat-eating, or *carnivorous.* Still others are *omnivorous;* they eat both plants and meat. Some live in trees, others on the ground, and still others, underground.

The pouches, made of skin, are always attached to the outside of the abdomen. Some pouches are deep, others shallow. Some are fur-lined, others are not. Some pouches, like the kangaroo's, open at the top, toward the front of the animal. Others open toward the rear of the animal. Some pouches are just loose flaps of skin. But there is one thing all pouches have in common. They always cover the mother's nipples, where the babies' milk comes from.

The pouch is vital for survival because the babies are born before they are fully developed. At birth they are blind, hairless, and very tiny. Even the largest marsupials measure less than 1 inch (2.5 cm) and weigh less than 1 ounce (.03 kg) when they are born!

With unformed back legs, the pocket baby must make its way from the birth canal at the rear of the

The mouse opossum from Central America is one of the smallest marsupials.

The bilby, which looks like a rabbit, is an endangered species.

mother's body to the pouch. Relying on its front legs, the baby pulls itself by instinct through its mother's fur. It needs the protection of the pouch where it can feed on its mother's milk until it grows big and strong enough to fend for itself.

Other mammals, including dogs, cats, and people, have completely formed eyes, ears, legs, and so on when they are born. They are called placental mammals. Instead of a pocket, the mother has a placenta inside her womb that nourishes the baby until birth. By that time, the baby has developed to the point where it can be separated from its mother.

In a way, a marsupial baby is like a human infant that is born too early. A premature infant must be put into an incubator to keep it warm and protected until it gains the strength to live on its own. A marsupial's pouch serves the same purpose as an incubator.

Most marsupials live in Australia. Australia is a very large island on the other side of the world from the Americas. Because it is in the southern hemisphere, its summer months occur when North America is having winter. Australia has mountains, deserts and plains, cities and farms. It is so huge and varied that it's considered a continent.

Why are marsupials concentrated in Australia? Scientists believe that millions of years ago, Australia was part of a large land mass that included what is now known as Africa, South America, and Antarctica. Then Australia broke away and became an island, and the marsupials living there became cut off from many other animals. Because they did not have to compete for food and space with a lot of other animals, they thrived.

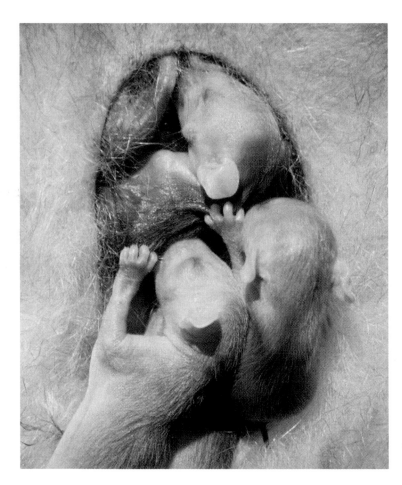

An opossum's pouch opens to the rear. The babies begin leaving the pouch when they become too big for it.

Many of the marsupials living outside Australia probably could not survive changes in climate that occurred as the land shifted. Also, they may not have been able to survive the competition with other animals, including man. Only the opossum of the Americas and a South American ratlike marsupial withstood these challenges.

Placental mammals have been much more successful than marsupials outside Australia. Scientists think placental mammals may have evolved from marsupials. If that's true, a womb is just a highly developed pouch.

So the island environment of Australia has protected marsupials. Their evolution has slowed down. Without much competition, marsupials have not had to adapt or evolve. Other animals go through many changes over the eons and look quite different today from their ancestors. But through millions of years, marsupials have undergone very little change.

However, in the last few centuries marsupials have had to deal with a new threat. Europeans began hunting large numbers of them when they first came to Australia in the eighteenth century. Some marsupials became extinct or endangered. Fortunately, in this century Australia began protecting its precious pocket babies. Australians realize that there is nothing else like them on earth.

The Opossum: The American Marsupial

Opossums have been on earth since the time of the dinosaurs. They are quite unique creatures, for they are the only marsupials to survive in large numbers outside Australia. There are sixty-five opossum species, more than any other family of marsupial. Opossums and a tiny family of ratlike marsupials in South America are the only marsupials native to the Americas.

In the United States, there is the common opossum, also known as the Virginian opossum. Long ago, it was found mostly in the southern states, but it gradually moved north into Canada.

Baby opossums climb on their mother's back when they leave the pouch.

When little opossums are born, they are exceedingly tiny, no larger than an eraser on a pencil. They are blind, earless, pink, and naked. They weigh so little that it would take twenty of them to weigh as much as a dime. Their back legs are like little tiny clubs. They use their more developed front feet to climb through the mother's fur to the pouch on her abdomen. The very strong ones reach the pouch in less than a minute.

Inside the pouch, the baby takes a nipple into its tiny mouth and holds fast. It holds so tightly that its mouth almost melds with the nipple. A mother opos-

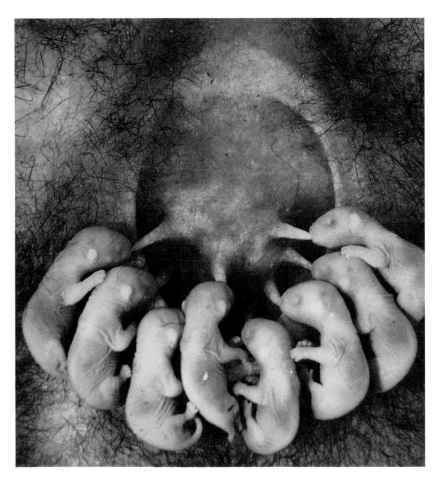

Inside the pouch, babies cling tightly to a nipple for eight weeks before letting go.

sum can feed from nine to seventeen babies, but the average number in one litter is twelve or thirteen. If more babies are born than the mother can nurse, she casts some of them out of the pouch. The lucky ones stay attached to the nipples for about eight weeks until their organs develop.

At nine weeks of age, each baby begins to climb in and out of the pouch and ride on its mother's back, clinging to her fur. By the time it is fourteen weeks old, the baby no longer needs to be nursed and starts to find its own food. It has also learned to climb trees, to hide from enemies, and to fight if necessary. It won't be much longer before it can live on its own.

THE WILY OPOSSUM

Grown opossums have pointed white faces with large, gleaming black eyes. The name "opossum" comes from an Indian word meaning "white face." Opossums have a pink nose and hairless thin ears that can be folded over the ear openings when they sleep. They have a good sense of smell and good eyesight, especially at night.

Springing up through their rough grayish fur are long white hairs. These are called guard hairs because they keep the fur from becoming worn.

Opossums have dark feet with pink toes. On the front feet are five toes with claws. On the back feet are four toes with claws and a fifth without. This odd toe is like a thumb. It allows the opossum to grasp a tree branch or hold food as we do with our hands. Because of this "thumb," the opossum footprint is different from that of any other animal.

The common opossum grows to be about 40 inches (101 cm) long, including its long tail. Adult males weigh 6 to 7 pounds (2 to 2.7 kg), and females weigh 4 to 5 pounds (1.8 to 2.2 kg).

The tail of the opossum is rough and scaly to give it a good grip on tree branches. This kind of tail is called *prehensile*, which means it is good for wrapping around

A young opossum can hang from branches by its prehensile tail.

and grasping things. Occasionally, young opossums hang by their tails from tree limbs, but adults are too heavy to hang. They use their tails mostly for holding onto limbs and balancing in trees.

Opossums are omnivorous; they eat any kind of food. They can feast on fruit or snails, acorns or mice, grasshoppers or earthworms, seeds, lizards, or frogs. Sometimes, they are even cannibals; they eat other opossums that have been killed.

They have fifty teeth, more than any other North American mammal. Some of them are biting teeth, some are long canine teeth, and others are chewing teeth. Their jaws can open as wide as 180 degrees.

Opossums don't like extreme weather. Those in northern regions cannot hibernate like bears do, but in below-zero temperatures, they stay in their dens for days at a time. When they get desperately hungry, they go out into the cold to hunt for food.

In warmer places, opossums cool themselves by licking their paws and rubbing their fur. In very hot weather, they like to go swimming. If a mother opossum has tiny babies in her pouch, she can still swim. She simply closes her pocket by tightening the muscles around its rim, much like we do when we clamp our mouths shut. The little babies in the pouch are safe from the water. They need very little oxygen, so the air in the pouch is enough for them.

The homes of opossums can be found in many places. Sometimes opossums move into a hollow tree or log or an uprooted tree stump. They line the space inside with dried leaves gathered in their curled tails. Or they may take over the abandoned burrows of other animals. They travel around a lot and change homes frequently.

Opossums like to live near the water, in places that are wooded or swampy. When they are adults, they usually live by themselves.

When an opossum is frightened, it runs away or escapes up a tree. But if it is cornered, it hisses and shows its long teeth. If that does not stop its attacker, the opossum just falls over and plays dead. Its body goes limp, its front paws clench into balls, and its mouth hangs open. It can be poked, kicked, pushed and even bitten by a dog without showing any sign that it is still alive. When the danger is over, it simply gets up and walks away.

This remarkable trick may be one reason opossums have survived where other marsupials have not. People sometimes copy this sneaky behavior by pretending to be asleep. This is known as "playing possum."

Opossums can live up to seven years, but their average life span is two or three years. The main cause of death today is the automobile. Opossums freeze when they see an oncoming car approach. They just stand still. This is one situation where playing dead doesn't work. Cars run over thousands of them every year.

This opossum is pretending to be dead to fool an attacker.

Opossums were often hunted for food in the past, and opossum furs were sold in great numbers to Europe. However, opossum is considered a poor quality fur.

The common opossum is the only marsupial in the United States. It also lives in other parts of North, Central, and South America. But there are many other marsupials living in the Americas outside the United States.

MARSUPIALS OF LATIN AMERICA

There are at least forty species of mouse opossums in Mexico, Central America, and South America. They are often found in banana plantations and on vines.

As you might expect, they are much smaller than the common opossum. They may be as small as a mouse or as large as a rat. Most have markings on their faces, short velvety fur, and a prehensile tail. Some of the smaller mouse opossums have no pouch—only a flap of skin. But just like other opossums, the babies hold fast to the nipples while nursing.

Shrew opossums live in South America. As their name suggests, they are shrewlike, with tiny eyes and pointed faces. They are small, about the size of mouse opossums. The smallest known shrew opossum lives in Brazil and is less than 3 inches (7.6 cm) long.

The woolly opossum got its name because of its dense fur. It has bright orange eyes and a dark stripe down the center of its face. This opossum is about 10 inches (25 cm) long. Instead of a pouch, it has just two flaps of skin. It lives in Central America and the northern and central parts of South America.

Slightly smaller than the common opossum of the United States is the four-eyed opossum. It gets its name from the large white spots circled in black above its eyes. It looks as if the animal has four eyes. The spots confuse its enemies, keeping them from striking at its real eyes.

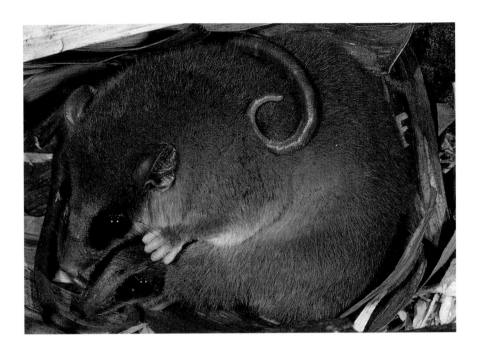

This Mexican mouse opossum lives in Costa Rica.

from the large white spots circled in black above its eyes. It looks as if the animal has four eyes. The spots confuse its enemies, keeping them from striking at its real eyes. Four-eyed opossums live in trees in nests of dried leaves and grass. They are active only at night, and they feed on a wide variety of plants and animals.

Four-eyed opossums can be found from Mexico to Argentina. The variety that lives in Central America has a rather crude pouch, which opens to the front. In South

The two white spots over the eyes of the four-eyed opossum look like an extra pair of eyes.

America, the four-eyed opossum has no pouch, just flaps of skin.

Then there is the yapok. It is also called a water baby, or water opossum, because it spends time in water as well as on land. It has webbed back feet and waterproof fur. It catches clams, crayfish, and water insects in the water. To eat them, it leaves the water and sits down on land. The mother's pouch opens toward the back, and it closes tightly when the mother is in the water. Yapoks range from southern Mexico to Argentina.

The Koala: Australia's Sweetheart

One of the best-loved marsupials in Australia is the koala. Koalas are sometimes called koala bears, but they are not even related to bears. They are cousins of kangaroos and opossums and have pocket babies as other marsupials do.

But koalas do look a lot like little bears. They have plump little bodies and stubby tails that are practically invisible. They have teddy-bear faces with round furry ears. Their eyes are bright and dark and their noses look like shiny, rubbery leather. Though their fur is usually a misty gray color, some koalas are brownish or yellowish. An extra layer of

A baby koala rides on its mother's back.

fat on their little rumps gives koalas some cushioning for sitting all day on hard tree branches.

Eastern Australia is the only place koalas live, outside of zoos. The largest koalas live toward the southern end of Australia, and the smallest live in the northern end.

When a young koala is born, it is less than 1 inch (2.5 cm) long. It stays in its mother's pouch for about six months. By that time, it is about 10 inches (25 cm) tall and has fur all over its body. After leaving the mother's pouch, the koala crawls up onto her back. It rides around on her back until it is a year old, when it is almost full grown. Koalas are between 2 and 3 feet (.6 and .9 cm) tall when they are grown.

FOOD AND DRINK FROM THE EUCALYPTUS

Koalas almost never drink water. Because of this peculiarity, the aborigines, the native people of Australia, named them *koala*, which means "one who never drinks." Koalas get the water they need by licking dew off the leaves they eat.

The major food koalas eat is the tough, oily leaf of the eucalyptus tree. They have two very sharp front teeth to tear the leaves from the stems. They chew the leaves with their back teeth.

Eucalyptus trees are a type of gum tree. Koalas also eat the leaves from other gum trees, including tallow-wood, scrubby gum, and red gum. Gum trees are a source of medicines. In fact, the oil from gum trees make koalas smell like medicine. That is why fleas and lice don't bother them.

Koalas must be very careful about which type of gum tree they eat from. During certain seasons, the oil in the leaves changes into an acid. If koalas were to eat the acid,

A mother koala teaches her baby which leaves are safe to eat.

they could be poisoned. To avoid this danger, they regularly change from one type of tree to another.

Mother koalas can tell when the oil has changed to acid by sniffing the leaves and tasting them. A mother always checks the leaves before letting her little ones eat from a tree. If the leaves are not safe, she takes her young to another tree. As young koalas grow, they learn from their mothers which leaves are good to eat.

If you met a koala in the daytime, it would probably stare back at you. It would look sleepy and bored because it stays awake all night, like a bat or an owl does. Animals that are active at night are called *nocturnal*. Koalas do their eating at night. Sometimes they eat almost all night long. They just keep filling their mouths until their cheeks puff out. When daylight comes, they snuggle into the fork of a tree and go to sleep.

The koala mother teaches her little ones to climb and gives many other koala lessons. She teaches them to behave well. When she thinks they are being naughty, she turns them over, and gives them a sound spanking. The youngsters scream and cry, sounding very much like human children. After a while, the mother usually puts her arms around the crying koala, and they take a nap together.

Young koalas walk slowly and heavily. When full grown, they can walk for miles in the dark to look for food. Koalas are very good climbers since they spend a lot of time in trees. They can also swim across streams, but they can't run very well. They don't fight very well, either, so they seem rather helpless. Yet if cornered, they strike out with their strong, sharp claws.

Even though koalas are usually peaceful animals, some of them can be grouchy. A koala learns at a young age that its older relatives don't like living close to one another. Each likes to have its own tree to eat from, and its own tree to sleep in. When young koalas go into trees that are already occupied, the older koalas gruffly chase them away.

SAVING THE TEDDY BEAR

Koalas are harmless animals. They do not hurt people or kill other animals. They never destroy gardens or flowers. They are gentle and trusting. If you ever got a chance to hold one, you would find that it is very friendly. It might even cuddle close and put its arms around your neck.

Koalas never seem to be afraid. When people approach, they don't try to hide, and they sit in bare trees where they can easily be seen. They also walk across open highways with little concern for oncoming cars.

Because of this, koalas flourished on their island paradise. At one time, there were millions of koalas in Australia. But the number of koalas began declining early

Koalas are affectionate, trusting animals.

in this century when hunters shot large numbers of them for their soft fur.

Many hundreds of koalas were lost in bush fires, too. Bush fires are sudden fires that spread through the vegetation of Australia. The oily leaves of the gum trees make the flames spread fast.

Also, as towns grew and farms spread out, the land

was cleared of forests. Many of the gum trees that koalas need to live were destroyed.

Fortunately, Australia passed a law to stop the hunting. The country also set aside sanctuaries for the koalas. The sanctuaries are special parks where they are safe. The people who run the parks make sure there are plenty of gum trees for the koalas.

Outside Australia, you can see koalas in some zoos, but not in all. That is because eucalyptus and other gum trees can grow only in warm climates. In the United States, California has a suitable climate for gum trees. However, even though Illinois is not warm enough to grow the trees, the Lincoln Park Zoo in Chicago has several koalas. The eucalyptus leaves are flown in daily from Florida, where gum trees can grow.

If you visit a zoo, make sure you see the koalas if it has them. You will discover why they are called "Australia's sweethearts."

Possums, Bandicoots, and Numbats: Small Australian Marsupials

Australia has many marsupials smaller than koalas. The smallest are the pouched mice. The dunnart is a pouched mouse that lives in dry areas. It has large ears and narrow feet. It stores fat in its tail, and when food is scarce, it lives on the fat. Mother dunnarts have from six to ten babies in a litter.

Another marsupial mouse is the wuhl-wuhl. It is a type of jerboa marsupial mouse, with long ears and a little tuft on the end of its tail. Its legs are long and skinny like a kangaroo's. But instead of hopping, it gallops. The mother wuhl-wuhl carries six to eight babies in a pouch that opens to the rear.

This fat-tailed dunnart has babies nursing underneath.

Still another marsupial mouse is called the mulgara. It has a crest of stiff hairs on its tail and is as large as a small rat. Mulgaras often bask in the sun like lizards do. And before eating, mulgaras always clean themselves carefully.

Although they rarely fight, mulgaras threaten each other a lot. Sitting upright, they open their mouths, lean forward until their noses touch, and then jerk back and begin threatening again.

Another very common pouched mouse is the tuan. It is about the size of a squirrel and lives in trees in nests lined with grass and leaves. It eats insects, birds, and at times, other small animals. It can be a fierce little fighter, but some people have been able to tame very young ones and keep them as pets. Mother tuans care for three to six babies in a saucer-shaped pouch. The babies leave the shallow pouch when they are four months old.

SUCKING AND FLYING POSSUMS

The Australian possum got its name because it looks like the American opossum. But other than being marsupials, they are quite different. Australian possums do not play dead, nor do they eat everything under the sun, as the American opossum does. With fewer teeth than the American opossum, the Australian possum eats only plant life. Another difference is that Australian possums live in trees and have feet like koalas.

One tiny possum, about the size of a mouse, is known as the noolbenger. It is sometimes called the "honey possum" or the "honey sucker" because it feeds on the nectar of flowers as bees and hummingbirds do. It has a long nose and long tongue. If it is difficult to get at the flowers, the noolbenger hangs by its whiplike tail and eats until full. Noolbengers like to dine at night in the company of other noolbengers, but they like to live alone.

Members of the flying possum family have a thin piece of skin stretching between the front and back feet on each side. When they spread their four legs, they look as if they have wings. They don't really fly, but they leap from high places and glide through the air. Though grace-

The honey possum feeds on the nectar of flowers.

ful and agile in the air, they are clumsy on the ground. They waddle as they walk.

One small flying possum, about 7 inches (17.7 cm) long, is called the sugar glider. It has the same taste for sweets that the noolbenger does. It feeds on flowers and leaves, and gashes the bark of trees to lick up the sap that leaks out.

Mother sugar gliders have only one or two babies at a time. They stay in the pouch for about four months feeding on milk. But when they are through nursing, they begin looking for sweets.

Pygmy possums are mouse-size. They have dense

The extra skin on either side of the sugar glider acts like wings when it leaps from high places.

fur but hairless ears. They feed on insects and lizards, holding them in their front paws as squirrels do. When insects are scarce during the cold months, they live off fat stored in their tails. They make nests of leaves high up in the trees, and sleep in them in groups with their tails curled tightly around them and their ears folded down.

Pygmy gliders, also known as feather-tail gliders or pygmy flying possums, are similar to other flying marsupials. But they are so small that you could hold five or six in your hand.

The spotted cuscus looks somewhat like a cat.

A possum found on many islands around Australia is the spotted cuscus. It has a stocky build and is about as big as a cat. It may have green, yellow, orange, or brown bulging eyes with yellow rings around them. Its ears are small and almost hidden in its dense fur. The fur can be any color from off-white to almost black, but it always has white spots.

The cuscus live in trees, sleep all day, and feed at night on insect and bird eggs. When they have been

If they get inside houses, brush-tailed possums can be destructive.

raised in or near villages, they can become very tame. But if disturbed, they can fight with tooth and claw. The cuscus is often hunted for its meat and fur.

Closely related to the cuscus is the common brush-tailed possum. It is found all over Australia in forests, deserts, and rocky places. These possums are as big as foxes and have dense, woolly dark fur. They eat mainly vegetation, but they also like almonds and rose petals.

Having adjusted well to civilization, brush-tails thrive near towns. But if they get into a house, they can be very destructive. And when their dens are disturbed, they defend them very well. They show their anger by opening their mouths wide, hissing, and making clicking sounds. If that doesn't scare the enemy away, brush-tails fight fiercely. But people who have tamed them say they make affectionate pets.

Other possums include the ring-tailed possum and the striped possum. Ring-tailed possums were so-named because they curl their tails into one or two rings. And striped possums have white stripes running from nose to tail like a skunk does.

JUMPING BANDICOOTS

Another well-known group of marsupials are the bandicoots. They live in forests and woodlands throughout

The long-nosed bandicoot looks like a rat.

Australia and nearby islands. They may be as small as a rat or as large as a rabbit. But they look more like badgers, with long pointed noses and brownish-gray fur. Their sharp claws help them dig for food, such as earthworms, insects, bulbs, and roots.

If disturbed, bandicoots gallop away. They can also jump straight up in the air, swing around, and speed away in another direction.

There are several kinds of bandicoots. One called the bilby is about the size of a cat and has long ears and a bushy tail. Bilbies eat insects and meat. They are the only bandicoots that dig burrows and crawl into them to escape the heat during the day. When they sleep, they tuck their heads between their front feet and fold their ears down over their faces.

Other bandicoots include a ratlike bandicoot that has pointed ears and a long nose. Another, plumper bandicoot has round ears and a short nose.

Mother bandicoots have six, eight, or more nipples in a pouch that opens to the back. But they usually have only two babies at a time.

EVEN STRANGER MARSUPIALS

The numbat is a small marsupial with dark stripes on its face. It has a long, pointed snout, a long, slender tongue, and a long, somewhat bushy tail. Because it feeds mainly on termites and other insects, it is often called the marsupial anteater.

Numbats are unusual in that the female has no real pouch. However, baby numbats attach themselves to the mother's four nipples for many months as other pocket babies do. They are protected somewhat by the mother's long hair.

Perhaps the oddest of all the marsupials is the marsupial mole that lives in the deserts of Central Australia. This mole is blind because its eyes are covered by skin. Since it lives underground, it doesn't need to see.

The mole digs a hole and dives in, "swimming" in the sand about 3 inches (7.6 cm) below the surface. Every once in a while it comes up for air for a short time. Above ground, it scoots along on its stomach, pushing with its back feet.

Marsupial moles are about the size of rats, with short, naked tails. They can be any color from creamy white to reddish gold. Their short front legs have feet like paddles, and flat, scooplike claws for digging. Their ears, which can be closed, are only holes hidden by fine, silky fur. A hard shell protects their muzzles as they push through the sand.

These moles eat earthworms and whatever else they can find in the dirt. When times become very hard for marsupial moles, they can sink into an unconscious state. This state helps them live through crises.

The mother mole has only one baby at a time, even though she has a well-developed pouch. It opens to the back.

The marsupial mole may be far from nice-looking, but it is a friendly animal. It is so small and mild-mannered that you could hold one in your hand.

Wombats, Cats, and Devils: Middle-size Marsupials

There are many pocket babies about the same size as koalas living in Australia and its surrounding islands. One of the best known of this group are the wombats. The name came from an aborigine word that sounds like "womba" or "womat."

A baby wombat is very tiny, naked, and pink when it is born. Like other marsupials, it crawls through its mother's fur to her pouch and immediately begins nursing. A mother wombat can't feed more than two babies at a time. But after awhile even two babies become too much for the pouch. As they grow, they become so heavy that the pouch drags on the ground. Usually only one baby survives.

A wombat has a body like a pig's, but it can run very fast.

The survivor grows slowly. Its eyes open at four months, and a month later, its fur starts to come in. The pouch opens backward; a baby wombat peeking out of it would see where it has been, not where it's going. If you were to walk behind a mother wombat, you might see two bright eyes staring at you from between her back feet. At seven months, the baby becomes too large and heavy for the pouch. It begins to venture out of the pouch and to eat grass. But it still occasionally returns to the pocket to nurse.

At times little wombats act very silly. Full of fun, they run around their mothers, jumping on their backs and bumping them with their foreheads. They like to roll down hills, too, but they always stay close to their mothers. At anywhere from eight to ten months of age, they leave the pouch for good.

Adult wombats have heavy, chunky bodies with very short tails hidden in fur. They amble along on short legs, making murmuring sounds as they go. But they can run fast—up to 25 miles (40 km) an hour. They also have very good hearing and eyesight. Because they are burrowing animals, wombats have strong scooplike claws on four of the toes on each foot. A fifth toe has no claw at all.

Wombats dig tunnels up to 100 feet (30.5 m) long. At the end of the tunnel, they clear an area for sleeping and line it with dry leaves. They sleep in the burrow during the day and come out at night to eat. They feed on bark and roots, coarse grasses, rushes, and sedge, which are swamp plants. The roughness of their diet constantly wears down their teeth. Fortunately, their teeth never stop growing, so they never completely wear away.

There are two kinds of wombats. The common one has grayish-brown, coarse fur and a hairless nose. It lives in southeastern Australia and on a nearby island called Tasmania. The other wombat has just about the same fur color, but its nose is covered with fine hair. It is found in southern Australia.

These hairy-nosed wombats often dig several tunnels that connect under the ground. In sandy areas, they burrow beneath tree roots or a rocky ledge so that the top of the tunnel will not cave in. The tunnels become home for a rather crowded community of wombats.

Hairy-nosed wombats clean themselves by rolling in the dirt.

In some places where there is very little rain, the hairy-nosed wombats don't drink much water. Like koalas, they get their moisture from the plants they eat. With no water, they must clean themselves by clawing often through their fur, and by taking dust baths. They roll around in the dirt and then shake very hard to get rid of the dust, which takes oil and insects with it.

Wombats can be annoying because they are curious and like to snoop, but they are friendly toward people. The worst enemies of wombats are foxes and wild dogs called dingos. Their best defense against these predators is to run for their burrows.

The burrow can also save wombats from bush fires. But if the fire burns off all vegetation in the area, they sometimes starve. Many are also killed by cars on the roads, and aborigines often spear them for food.

THE TEMPERAMENTAL TASMANIANS

The Tasmanian devil is a marsupial that lives on the island of Tasmania off the coast of Australia. Although Tasmanian devils don't look exactly like the cartoon character, they have the same fierce expression and blood-curdling scream. That is why they are called devils.

Mother devils have large litters of baby devils, sometimes as many as fifty. Each baby is only .25 inches (.6 cm) long! Still, one mother can nurse no more than four babies. So the first four to reach her pouch survive.

The pouch of a Tasmanian devil is well-developed and opens to the rear. The mother closes it tightly as she moves through thickets of dense forest or when she goes swimming. After fifteen weeks, the baby devils leave the pouch. They don't leave because of overcrowding like other pocket babies do, but because it gets too hot for them in the pocket. Then they stay in a leaf-lined nest, though they go back to the pocket to nurse several times a day. They often tag along with their mother, sometimes riding on her back clinging to her fur.

Tasmanian devils have a bloodcurdling scream.

Full-grown Tasmanian devils are the size of a very large house cat. Their bodies are about 2 feet (.6 m) long, and they have 1-foot (.3 m)-long tails. Their heads are very large. Shaggy black hair covers their bodies, except for a white marking on the chest.

Devils are very noisy and quick-tempered, often flying into sudden rages. They have enormous appetites that never seem to be satisfied. At one feeding, they can consume over five times their own weight. To satisfy their hunger, they eat just about anything. They hunt other animals, and they scavenge for rotting food that other animals will not eat. With forty-two grinding teeth and strong jaws, they can easily tear apart birds and lizards. They can even crush the skull of a sheep. What's more, they sometimes eat other devils.

They do not fight each other often, but when they do, it is to the death. And the winner eats the loser. Fortunately, they are not known to attack people.

Their incredible appetite may cause mother devils to accidentally eat their own offspring! If one of her children comes near her in the dark, she may not recognize it and may attack it. To prevent this, the mothers typically spit on their paws and rub the saliva onto their young ones' heads when they stop nursing. Then if one comes near its mother in the dark, she will recognize the smell of the saliva and not attack it.

Fierce as Tasmanian devils are, some people claim that if trained as pets, they are clean, playful, and affectionate.

There are many kinds of marsupial cats in Australia and Tasmania. The largest of them, at 3 feet (.9 m) long, is the tiger cat. Its brown fur is covered with many irregularly shaped whitish spots, even on the tail. It is carnivorous, feeding on animals as large as small wallabies and rat kangaroos (see Chapter 6). It helps that it can open its mouth more than ninety degrees. Tiger cats make their homes in trees, and are most active at night.

These baby tiger cats will grow to the size of a large lynx.

Other marsupial cats, also known as native cats, are closer to the size of house cats. Native cats have less distinctive markings on the fur and tail than tiger cats do. Like the tiger cat, they hunt mainly at night. They live in several areas of Australia and nearby islands.

The native cats and the tiger cat give birth to large litters—sometimes as many as twenty-four tiny young. But the mothers usually have only six to eight nipples, so only the first few to reach the pouch survive.

Kangaroos, Wallabies, and Boodies: The Largest Marsupials

The kangaroo belongs to a group of marsupials called *macropads*, which means "big feet." These marsupials do indeed have unusually large feet. The kangaroo, the largest of the macropads, has feet that measure more than 10 inches (25 cm).

According to one legend, the name *kangaroo* comes from the words "kang guru." When the Europeans first came to Australia, aborigines frequently shouted those words when they saw a kangaroo leap out of the bushes. The phrase really means, "there he goes." But the first Europeans to hear it thought it was the animal's name.

Kangaroos hopping along a beach in Australia

There are many sizes of kangaroos in Australia. The three largest are the red kangaroo, the gray forester, and the wallaroo.

Even though some kangaroos may grow to be as tall as 6 feet (1.8 m), when a kangaroo is born, it is less than 1 inch (2.5 cm) long. It is hairless, blind, and underdeveloped, except for its front legs and paws. These are already formed and strong enough to pull it through its mother's hair to the pouch. Unlike the smaller marsupials, kangaroos have only one baby at a time. So the little kangaroo, also called a *joey*, has the pouch all to itself.

For three months, while it nurses, the red joey grows very slowly. When it is fifteen weeks old, its growth speeds up. Soon after, the joey begins exploring the outside world by poking its head and forelegs out of the pouch as the mother ambles about.

At six months of age, the red joey has a coat of fur and is ready to leave the mother's pouch. Although still nursing occasionally, it begins to eat grass. Gradually the young joey stays outside the pouch more and more, but continues to snuggle down in it to sleep at night.

At eight months, when the red joey is too large to fit in the pouch, the mother evicts it for good. She cuffs the youngster until it understands that it cannot return to the pouch. Afterward the joey stays close to its mother, hopping alongside her. If danger threatens or if the youngster starts to wander, she gives a warning by thumping her joey with her huge back foot.

A young red joey returns to the pouch to nurse.

The red kangaroo lives on the hot plains of Australia. Its name comes from the reddish color of the male; the female is blue-gray. Red kangaroos are herbivorous, grazing on grass and herbs. They usually eat at twilight. During the heat of the day, they rest in the shade. Or they may scrape away the hot top soil and make a cool hollow to lie in. They also cool themselves by licking their front legs and paws, where there is less hair than other areas of their bodies.

The red kangaroos have adapted well to the dry plains. They are good at withstanding heat and thirst. Like camels, they can go without water for weeks, getting moisture from the plants they eat.

The gray forester kangaroo is a lot like the red kangaroo, but it lives in wooded areas of southern and eastern Australia and the island of Tasmania. It is about the same size as the red kangaroo. However, the gray joey doesn't leave the pouch until it is eight months old. It goes in and out of the pouch for the following three months and nurses until the age of one year.

The wallaroo is the third large kangaroo. It has a strong, solid body covered with long coarse hair. Also known as the hill kangaroo, or rock kangaroo, it lives all over Australia in gullies and outcrops of rock. But to get the vegetation it lives on, it must go down to the plains at night to eat.

A good way to tell the three large kangaroos apart is

to look at their noses. The gray forester has a rim of black skin around its nostrils, which are separated by fur. The red kangaroo also has black-rimmed nostrils, but the area between them is bare. The wallaroo has a plain black, naked nose.

A large kangaroo can travel 30 to 40 miles (48 to 64 km) an hour, taking leaps of up to 25 feet (7.6 m). They have to be fast because flight is their best chance of survival when faced with an enemy.

Kangaroos like family life and live in groups called mobs. Often, the mob is headed by a mature male known as a boomer. Unless provoked, kangaroos never start a fight with outsiders. Most of their fighting takes place among themselves when males fight over females.

Kangaroos always move their back feet together

except when swimming. Although they can swim well, they don't go into the water very often. It usually happens only when they are being chased or when they are escaping a bush fire. A kangaroo uses its front paws just like hands. Its strong thick tail can be used as a prop when it sits down. It can also support the kangaroo during a fight when it raises both back feet and uses them as weapons.

At one time, hunters killed kangaroos and sold their hides for leather and their meat for pet food.

WALLABIES

Wallabies are also macropads, but their feet are less than 10 inches (25 cm) long. They have the same build and carry their babies in the same way as the large kangaroos. So they are considered kangaroos, only their size is medium rather than large.

Wallabies are found throughout Australia and Tasmania. Some of them live in swampy areas, and others in the dry interior.

The true, or brush, wallabies have deerlike ears, long narrow feet, and long tapered tails. They come in many different colors. Brush wallabies live in tall brush areas, where they can feed on grasses. One species, the pretty-face wallaby, has light gray fur and white stripes on its face. A white stripe also runs from hip to hip under the tail.

The pretty-face wallaby lives in grassy areas.

Other wallabies spend most of their time in trees. These tree wallabies, or tree kangaroos, are fine climbers. They have shorter back feet than other kangaroos and instead of tapering, the tail is thick along its entire length. The fur around the neck forms a ruff, a sort of a frilly collar. When nestled in a tree during a storm, the wallaby sits with its head down, and the rain runs over the ruff, missing the rest of its body.

Unlike other animals, tree wallabies do not climb down from tree branches; they simply jump off them. These kangaroos are commonly found in New Guinea, an island just north of Australia.

Another group of wallabies are known as whiptail

or nail-tailed wallabies because they hold their long slender tails upright when hopping. They live in large groups in both grassy and wooded areas of eastern Australia.

The black-tail wallaby, also known as the swamp wallaby, likes swampy areas. Its coloring depends on where it lives. In southwestern Australia, the tammar wallaby lives in dense thickets. The conditions in this region are hard and very dry. Tammar wallabies survive by drinking sea water. Most animals cannot tolerate salt water, but it does not harm these wallabies. They belong to a group called the scrub wallabies.

Kangaroos and some wallabies are the largest of the macropads. There are many smaller ones, such as the hare wallaby, which is the size of a rabbit. It also has ears like a rabbit's.

The smallest macropads are rat kangaroos. They are about 12 inches (30 cm) long. They look like rats except for their kangaroo-like back legs. One of this group is the potoroo. Potoroos live in forest areas where there is lots of rainfall, and they feed on insects and plants.

Many rat kangaroos make nests on the ground. However, at least one species digs burrows and lives in groups underground. This species belongs to a group of rat kangaroos called boodies. Boodies are known for the way they fight with each other. You might laugh if you saw it; they lie on their sides and kick at each other with their back feet. Boodie babies stay in their mother's pouch for only about four months.

The rat kangaroo is not really a kangaroo, but it has large back feet like a kangaroo.

There are many more macropads and other marsupials than those mentioned here. Very little is known about some of them. But all of them, from the tiny pouched mouse to the tallest kangaroo, are strange creatures indeed. What sets them apart from other animals is the way they carry their young — those little ones we fondly call "pocket babies."

Glossary

aborigines—the natives of Australia, the first people to live there. Most Australians are not aborigines, but are descendants of Europeans, who first came to Australia in the eighteenth century.

boomer—a male kangaroo that heads a group of kangaroos called a mob.

carnivorous—eating meat, or animals, rather than plants.

dingo—a reddish-brown wild dog that lives in Australia.

extinct—no longer existing on earth. Species of animals can become extinct.

herbivorous—eating plants and vegetables, rather than meat.

joey—a baby kangaroo.

macropads—a family of marsupials that includes kangaroos, wallabies, and rat kangaroos.

marsupials—an order of mammals that includes kangaroos, opossums, koalas, and other animals that raise their babies in pockets, or pouches.

mob—a group of kangaroos that live together like a family.

nocturnal—describes an animal that is active at night, rather than during the day.

omnivorous—eating both plants and animals.

placenta—the lining of the uterus, or womb. It nourishes the babies of nonmarsupials before they are born.

placental mammals—mammals whose babies grow inside their bodies in the uterus, or womb.

prehensile—describes rough and scaly tails that are good for grabbing and wrapping around branches.

For Further Reading

Barrett, Norman. *Kangaroos and Other Marsupials.* New York: Franklin Watts, 1991.

Burt, Denise. *The Birth of a Koala.* Novato, Calif.: Terra Nova, 1988.

Crowcroft, Peter. *Australian Marsupials.* New York: McGraw-Hill, 1972.

Jenkins, Marie. *Kangaroos, Opossums, and Other Marsupials.* New York: Holiday House, 1975.

McClung, Robert. *Possum.* New York: William Morrow, 1963.

Rue III, Leonard Lee. *Meet the Opossum.* New York: Dodd, Mead, 1983.

Wise, William. *Amazing Animals of Australia.* New York: Putnam, 1970.

Index